Closed for Business

Closed for Business

The Complete Collection of Steve Ward's Poetry

by

Steve Ward

With an Introduction by Don Briddell

 SkipJack Press

ISBN   1879535025

Several of these poems were originally published in:

The Crisfield Times
The Salisbury Times
The Baltimore Sun
The History of Crisfield and Surrounding Areas
on Maryland's Eastern Shore.

Printed in the United States of America

4 6 8 7 5 3

SkipJack Press
Ocean Pines, MD

C O N T E N T S

3   The Hopeless Romantic

4   Poetic Commentary

5   Verse Advise

6   The Last Poem

Colophon

ILLUSTRATIONS

The illustrations in this book were drawn by Jack Schroeder, a Crisfield artist, who is currently using the original Ward shop as his studio. All drawings are original to this book.

The illustration on the dust cover was drawn by Don Briddell. The photographs on the dust cover were taken by Jack Andrews.

INTRODUCTION

Steve Ward, along with his younger brother Lem, went far beyond his personal world of Crisfield, Maryland, to contribute significantly to American culture. These men, whose lives were tied to the waterman's life of the Chesapeake Bay, were the founders and foremost practitioners of an art form known as WILDFOWL CARVING. Without leaving home, they exposed thousands of people to the innate beauties of wildlife and native crafts. Like their father before them, they were linked to the water which dominated their lives and the lives of the whole community. It was natural that following the ways of the water led them to decoy carving, guided as they were by nature herself.

Their humble shop was located in Crisfield, at the marsh's edge along Jenkins Creek on a "neck" of land pointing southward towards the waters of the Chesapeake. Their shop was filled with ducks and geese of all descriptions: canvasbacks, pintails, widgeons, teal, and scaup. Canada geese, snow geese and brant lined the shelves in various stages of completion. Over the years, many thousands of people came to visit them. Visitors, such as I, would stare in awe and wonder at their marvelous work, not only gaining insight into carving, but meeting two grand gentlemen seasoned, like the wood they carved, in the rich and fragrant ways of easy, natural living.

The Ward Brothers often quoted the anonymous poem "Dumb Country Boy," as they sought to explain their persona, values, and the rewards of the life which the two brothers lived.

Dumb Country Boy

I'm just a dumb old country boy,
Who ain't so very smart.
And when I talk I get mixed up,
My gears are hard to start.
It seems I don't have many brains
Like other folk I know,
And when it comes to 'siety,
My dumbness there I show.

I find it don't take many brains
The best in life to gain,
It's not your wealth or who you are,
Prestige you might obtain.
It only takes just simple faith
Eternal life to find.
No matter who or where you are
There's grace for all mankind.

I went down to the jailhouse once
To witness for the Lord.
I told them how the Lord saved me
They sure looked mighty bored.
They nudged each other then they smiled
They all knew I was dumb.
But they stayed in and I walked out
When leaving time had come.

I'm still that same dumb country boy
I hope I'll always be.
Just dumb enough to trust the Lord
For all eternity,
And so I'll just keep traveling on,
With Jesus in my heart,
I'm just a dumb old country boy
Who ain't so very smart.

Anyone who knew Steve was always delighted to find that he had a keen wit. Steve was philosophical in nature, perceptive to life's subtleties, and aware of human ironies. Crisfielders are known for their unique ways of speaking and their innovative approach to dialogue. Words held a fascination for Steve that nearly approached his love for carving. He told me one time of a fellow who, in the days of early television, didn't have a set. Everyone else was watching and discussing the shows at the old store when someone asked the fellow, "Why don't you get yourself a TV? The line (power line) runs right by your house." The fellow responded without a pause, "There are a lot of things running by my house I can't get!" Steve loved that down-home wit.

Steve was the sort of person who, after reciting "Dumb Country Boy," would vanquish all doubts the listener may have had about his sophistication. He looked around this world and saw it for what it was, a world that was fragmented, distracted, and in a mostly confused state. Steve chose a course straight and true along the lines of his tradition without letting the world take over his life. He was content to live a simple, humble life. He didn't drive a car. A bicycle served his needs. He didn't maintain a checkbook, preferring to live as gathering, bartering and cash would allow. Life was not a grand scheme for acquisition. The only upward mobility Steve aspired to was toward God. He chose to remain in his place of contentment. He was not bothered by ambition. Being himself was all that he required. Undoubtedly he succeeded, in my eyes at least, for he stands out vibrantly as a man worthy of admiration.

He appreciated all the fuss the world was to make about his decoys, but he didn't rely on it. I have told the story many times about visiting him on his death-bed at the Veteran's Hospital and remarking how dismayed I was not to own a single one of his decoys. "You don't need'um," he responded. "They are just old blocks of wood."

He had no illusions. He could recognize a block of wood from the legend surrounding it. With hatchet and knife he carved thousands upon thousands of decoys in his lifetime. Though Lem did the decoratives and moved carving into a proper art form, it is upon Steve's prolific decoy making that their great fame rests. I've heard others criticize him for being content with the simple form of the decoy, and Steve was the first to admit he was not an artist. However, it is the contention of many that as time affords perspective, Steve's work will indeed be understood as art. Though other decoys may get higher prices because of their novelty and rarity, Steve's decoys are, nonetheless, considered to be the most beautiful and elegant ever produced. Fortunately for the collector, they are also the most abundant.

In the part of the country where he lived, Steve was a known conversationalist. He had views and opinions on most subjects. He enjoyed a discussion and often folks who came to Crisfield sought him out. Lem, on the other hand, was quite content to have Steve do the talking. Steve was very protective of Lem and often shielded him from disruptions that might have interfered with his painting. Lem had a seriousness about him, the kind common to the dedicated artist.

Steve could work anywhere. He constantly had his pockets stuffed with heads to whittle. Lem, however, never liked to be watched, hence Steve's work area was in front of Lem's. To reach Lem, you had to get by Steve. One large department store in Wilmington, Delaware, once asked them to come to the store and carve in the front window. "You'll sell a mess of decoys," they were promised. They both found the suggestion preposterous.

Later on when the public's dropping in became so regular, they posted a sign on their shop which read, "Closed for Business." It was typical of these men that they would find just the right words to tell folks that they had to close the door to get any work done. However, if you looked closely when you drove up, you'd notice the bottom edge of the pull shade raise up on one end. If you saw this, you would know Lem was peeking out to see who it was. Oh, how gratifying it was to hear his voice holler as you approached, "You just come on in boy!" They tried to get tough, but in the end they'd always accommodate people. Thus, their house, as it sat by the side of the road, was open to all. They had more friends than anyone I ever knew. I mean they had the kind of friends that sit and chat with ease. No appointments necessary. If they were out, as sure as the tide, they'd soon be back.

Steve lived the American Dream without having to fall asleep to do it. When he looked back on his life, he used to say," I lived the life of a millionaire without knowing it. I could come and go as I pleased, fish and hunt when I wanted." And so it was for the Ward brothers. Dinner was always available for the netting, hooking, catching, shooting, and gigging in the marsh and rivers. The backyard garden Steve maintained complimented the fish and fowl with greens and fresh vegetables. Cash came from cutting-hair in their barber shop and decoys took care of the rest.

Their barbershop had the touch of the unconventional as well. The mix of Jergen's after-shave, oil paints, and cedar wood scent is unique to the Ward Bothers and remembered indelibly by every nose that ever entered. The floors were covered with a mix of human hair and wood chips. When the barber chairs had no customers those two would be in them carving. And when someone would suggest fishing, they'd be off.

I know I tend towards romanticizing them, but I also

remember that their lives were filled with adversity. Lem's daughter, Ida, told of these hardships in her moving book, "The Story of Lem Ward," edited by Glenn Lawson, which was published in 1984 by Schiffer Publishing Ltd. The brothers struggled and went without things that are now considered basic necessities by modern folks. During the depression, when money didn't exist, they burnt decoys as the coal gave out; decoys any one of which today would buy truck loads of coal delivered. It is only now in the safety of present memories that we can look back without feeling anguish upon the stress of those times.

Steve was within walking distance of everything he needed. His world proper was called, "Down Neck," or "Byrdtown," or "Sackertown". It is a reach of lowlands surrounded on three sides by marshes, creeks and the Chesapeake Bay. He found it an ideal place to live. He knew every square inch of the area. What may look like boring flatlands was for him intensely interesting. Steve didn't need the whole world for a home. All he needed was a place. Down Neck and the marshes beyond offered all he could ask for. He showed me that beauty was a personal matter. I must have heard him say a million times: "Beauty is in the eye of the beholder." I can still hear him say it.

What I saw and learned from the Ward brothers, between 1957 at 13 years of age, and 1962 when I went off to college was to provide me with the foundation upon which I have based my life in the arts. All I needed to know about how to make a living, I knew by the time I was 15 years old. What I didn't know was that it would be feasible to make a living carving wildlife. Bird carving was not a respectable profession until very recently. Lem and Steve blazed the trail, pioneering a way of living that blended their economic and artistic needs.

The Ward brothers were not taken seriously until they

were in their sixties. Well, there were a few individuals in the country that saw what was going to happen, but generally and typically, the brothers did not become "respectable" until about the time Mr. DuPont (of DuPont Chemicals in Delaware) rolled into town in a big long Cadillac. He parked in the Ward's lane and ordered a pair of each and every waterfowl that travels the Atlantic flyway. He offered $1,000 each for a total of 76 birds. In Lem's words that was all the money he could possibly imagine. As life would have it, after the 16th carving Lem suffered a stroke and the project was abandoned.

By the mid 1950's, the days of service decoys had passed. Though these decoys remained hot collector's items, the leading edge of wildfowl carving interest had shifted from the working decoy of Steve to the decoratives of Lem. It is, however, a great mistake to consider Steve less a creator of beauty than Lem.

Steve dearly loved language. Finding a way to put down an experience and explain poetically what he found meaningful was his personal passion. He wrote on anything handy. When I was sorting through his shop after the brothers had passed on, poems in bits and pieces were found stuck around on nails and in nooks and crannies everywhere.

Steve had no more than a fifth-grade education. Yet, he was the only practicing poet I ever met while growing up. Both Lem and Steve used poetry philosophically to find a way of saying what they knew as truth. Their down-home attitude and understanding of life was often explained poetically. When they found a poem that "said it all," they would recite it like a chant.

There are two predominant themes in Steve Ward's poetry. On the one hand, Steve wrote about the glories of family, truth, God, virtues, and simplicity. On the other hand, he portrayed the evils of pride, vice, money, and pretentiousness. Both of these themes are found in the most common celebration in his poetry; that of life itself. Steve's poetry explored the Down Neck country, the fishermen, the cormorants, herring, hardheads, and shad, the Crisfield oyster fleet, the tongers from Tangier, the Hard Crab Derby Ball, an old decoy full of shot, the names of ghost ships and the ring of buoys in storm-blown waves, a baseball game, a lover buckling her skates, thinking about being on Kitty's Branch. They are honest poems, in honest language, expressing values so basic as to stand out like overalls and gumboots in a ballroom.

I n their later years the Wards often quoted "Remorse," by Truman P. Reitmeyer. It's the story of a hunter who gave up hunting after killing a mated pair of geese and watching them die. Steve and Lem grew up as hunters. They hunted for the table and valued their times afield greatly. Yet as they grew older and less dependent on the hunt, their compassion took hold and they put their guns aside. Without necessity, it was useless slaughter. The live bird became more important than the dead one. After all, they had spent a lifetime putting life in their carvings. Lem once remarked he regretted every bird he killed and that if he had the power, he'd breathe life back into every one of them.

Steve and Lem had this poem by Truman printed up on their personal stationery and freely distributed it to all. It is a testimony to their ability to change and respond to the inner voice that men of wisdom yearn to follow. Lesser men, even should the voice of wisdom call, would follow instead their habits to the grave.

Remorse

by Truman P. Reitmeyer

A hunter shot at a flock of geese that flew within his reach.
Two were stopped in their rapid flight and fell on the sandy beach.
The male bird lay at the water's edge and just before he died
He faintly called to his wounded mate and she dragged herself to his side.

She bent her head and crooned to him in a way distressed and wild
Caressing her one and only mate as a mother would a child.
Then covering him with her broken wing and gasping with failing breath
She laid her head against his breast, feeble honk, then death.

This story is true, though crudely told. I was the man in the case.
I stood deep in the drizzle and cold and the hot tears burned my face.
I buried the birds in the sand where they lay, wrapped in my hunting coat.
And I threw my gun and belt in the bay when I crossed in the open boat.

Hunters will call me a right poor sport and scoff at the thing I did;
But that day something broke in my heart. And, shoot again? God Forbid!

Perhaps Steve and Lem would object to my personal interpretation of their lives and values. But with what other brush can I paint them save with my own, showing them as I knew them? Everyone who came in touch with the Ward brothers has a personal reason for venerating them. Their gifts were multifold. They let you praise them as the greatest carvers in America, or call them "two dumb country boys." It really didn't matter.

The Ward brothers had long lives together forming a remarkable brotherhood. For the eight years Lem survived Steve's death, Lem commented he only had half his life left. One time when I was visiting with Lem after Steve was gone, I saw him in the open door of his shop leaning against the jamb for support and gazing off into the loblobly pines surrounding Jenkins Creek, repeat to no one in particular, "It's a cruel world. It's a cruel world, boy."

I'd seen them working together years before, spirited and animated. Chips flying from hatchet and knife, brushes hairless from hard use, paint tubes mangled, and shelves lined with decoys in various stages of completion. At last, with the elongated shadows of the years creeping over their careers as artists, their work grinding to a halt with Lem's stroke and then with Steve's blindness, their era came to an end. A wooden duck and a few lines of poetry may be pitiful replacements for living men, but like all images, words, objects, or recollections in the mind, they gave us a foothold on the near vertical cliff face upon which we struggle in life.

The carvings of Steve and Lem are now a part of the national heritage. They, and their work, are unique to the times in which they lived. They made their mark on our civilization.

Don Briddell
Mt. Airy, Maryland, 1991

STEYE WARD

xx

Uncle Steve's Poetry

When my uncle Steve died in Feburary of 1976, I found scattered around the floor of his shop, in drawers of his desk and in boxes of his personal treasures, all of his poems he had written - at least all I could find. There may be even more.

I was so excited to find these gems - many of which I had read, many which were printed in local papers - but many I never knew existed.

After his death, my dream was to see these poems published in book form for the world to see, but I knew I had neither the finances or the "know how" for such a project. So, I gave them to a friend, a friend of Dad's and a friend of Steve's and, I'm proud to say, a friend of mine, Don Briddell.

I was fed poetry from the early days of my youth. Dad (Steve's brother, Lem Ward) didn't write poetry, but both he and Steve recited it in every day parlance. Poetry was for them another way of speaking; a way to give beauty and elegance to thoughts and feelings. Uncle Steve would jot down a verse or two and ask my opinion as I sat fascinated by a man with so little education, but as he often told me, poetry comes from the heart and soul.

Some noble spirit once said, "The books of theologians gather dust upon my shelves, but the pages of the poets are stained with my fingers and blotted with my tears."

Uncle Steve's poetry moves me in just this way - with tears and with joy.

Ida Ward Linton,
December, 1991

Two Boys, Three 'Coys and a Musket

It all happened because two boys made up their minds not to let a kicking musket get the best of them, and to someday make a stool of decoys of their own.

An old lighthouse keeper gave me and my boyhood pal, Syke, a rusty single-barreled musket that would knock your teeth out, or as the old heads used to say, "kick the soda out of a bisquit and never break the crust." The skin that thing knocked off us would last any hospital a whole year for skin grafts. Everytime we shot it, we swore it would be the last, but we'd go right back the next day for one more blast just to keep in practice. If we didn't get knocked flat we figured we were sissies, so we loaded her up and took our medicine. Sometimes we were as dead as whatever we shot at!

Syke and I had no decoys, only three old unpainted things that looked like waterwitches. We were sitting in a blind one day and three witches were diving outside our "decoys," too far to shoot. I said, "Syke, what do you think they're thinking about now?" He said, "I know what they're thinking. They're thinking if we've got to put up with this all winter long we might as well get killed now and have it over with!"

We killed many a witch with that old musket. Or, scared 'em to death, I don't know which. For when the load caught on fire and went by his head, the witch knew he was a goner and gave up the ghost. But right there that day in the blind, plans were made to have the stool of decoys we had so often talked about, at all costs.

On a chopping block, we made something that we

hoped would resemble a mallard, but it looked more like a loon than anything else. Nobody had ever seen a duck like it around Crisfield, not even the old folks, so we decided it was a species that hasn't migrated down this far yet. We kept right on making it anyway, hoping someone would come along and identify it, but nobody ever did. One old fellow said it looked like a 'scovey crossed with a loon. We didn't know if it was a compliment or not, until we saw one and then we knew it wasn't!

In the month of March, 1911, my pal Syke was drowned in the Pocomoke Sound. He was only fifteen years old. Red headed and freckle faced and a heart of gold. If Mark Twain had known him, he wouldn't have written Tom Sawyer or Huckleberry Finn. I didn't get over that blow for a long, long time. I lost all desire for the stool of decoys, but about four or five years later I grew big enough so that dad would let me use his skiff, decoys and gun. And I started all over again, for I had never really given up making my own stool of decoys.

Then my brother, Lem, was big enough to get interested and take up carving. It wasn't too hard, for dad was good at making decoys and we learned plenty from him. We really started turning them out and selling some to local gunners in the neighborhood. We noticed all the decoys on the creek where we lived were round bottomed and rolled from side to side very badly, so we decided ours would be flat. We were the first ones to turn the heads in all directions, some high, some low, some sleepers, and it worked. We anchored some at the breast end and at the tail end and some at the side so they wouldn't all be in the same position, and it worked. Every gunner knows sometimes nothing will work. Some days ducks won't even decoy to their own kind. The only way to fool them is to go home and go to bed. That will work!

The 1920s and 1930s went by and Lem started making the fancy preening birds, and people started coming to our shop from all over the United States and Europe. There were seven cars from seven different states in the yard one day. We don't claim to be great carvers, just lucky ones who know enough to never be satisfied with the duck we made today. Make a better one tomorrow. Try to improve on each and every one, and when you feel a certain day is not your day, stop and take the day off.

If some people knock you, consider every knock from them the biggest kind of boost. It's what you learn after you know it all that counts. Two boys had a dream and that dream came true. You can make yours come true. Remember, the most important fellow in this world today is you. He's with you right to the end.

The poet Robert Service said, "anybody can quit, it's the keeping on going that's hard." Man's greatest enemy is himself—the others don't count.

(Originally published in "The Ward Foundation Magazine" with a selection from an article "Memories", by Steve Ward.)

Closed for Business

1 THE DREAMY EASTERN SHORE

Soft Crab Time in Crisfield

It's soft crab time in Crisfield,
 You can hear the hammers ring;
They are fitting up the skipjacks,
 It's the first sure sign of Spring.

Bottoms all are red with copper,
 Sides are white and washboards drab;
Sails of pearly white are streaming;
 For it's time for Crisfield crabs.

You can hear the hoops go ringing
 For they go up mighty fast.
You can hear the halyards singing
 In the wind beside the mast.

You can hear the crab gulls chatter
    As they circle, dip and scream.
For it's soft crab time in Crisfield–
    Soft crabs from the Crisfield streams.

Yes, it's soft crab time in Crisfield,
    And it brings a world of dreams
To go skimming o'er the water
    On a June night's moonlit stream.

It's Springtime in the woodlands
    Where all nature seems to rhyme;
It's Summer in the meadows,
    But in Crisfield, SOFT CRAB TIME.

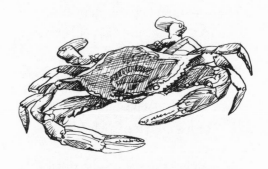

Signs of Spring

The fishermen are skinning bark
    from off their fish trap poles,
And boiling tar to smear the seine
    and patching up the holes.
The smell of copper fills the air
    and they all smile and sing,
For this is how the fishermen
    know that it is Spring.

They have to see no calendar to
    know that Spring is here,
For the Comorant are coming in
    from points both far and near.
And then too, a Fish Hawk circles
    gracefully above the foam
Screaming out his joyous message,
    "Spring is here, and I am home."

And the fishermen are driving
    poles as if they were all mad,
To trap the run of the Herring, the
    Hardheads and the Shad.
Although it is February and the
    cold nor'westers sing,
The fishermen are merry for they
    know that is is Spring.

All up and down the Chesapeake,
    the West and Eastern Shore,
From old Cape Charles way down
    the bay, clear up to Baltimore.
You can smell the tarpots boiling,
    you can hear the drawknives ring,
When the fishermen start toiling on
    their nets, you know it's Spring.

Crisfield Style

Put me off at Crisfield,
    For the Shad are on the run.
The Hard Heads right behind them,
    And boy, won't it be fun.
To ramble round the docks and boats,
    Where men know how to smile.
And taste Shad and Hard Heads,
    That are cooked in Crisfield style.

I want to see the Hard Heads and Shad
    Aflapping in a boat,
And smell them stewing, frying
    And taste them in my throat.
Baked Brown Shad for dinner,
    Stewed Hard Heads at night.
If there is one thing thing better
    Just keep it from my sight.

I want to hear those Tangier boys
    Laugh and sing and shout.
And hear Smith Parks kidding them,
    Just how to go about
Catching Shad and Hard Heads,
    Though they know it is a jest.
Yet when it comes to fishing,
    They know he is the best.

I want to watch the Sea Gulls,
    As they swoop down in a flash.
And gather up the fish that are thrown
    Overboard for trash.
I want to see the Fish Hawk
    As he gives his piercing scream,
And dives head first with talons spread
    In yonder tranquil stream.

So is it any wonder,
    That I am Crisfield bound.
Where everything that's good to eat
    Is in abundance found?
Stew up a pot of Hard Heads,
    Spuds, onion tops, and dough.
Or baked Shad served with corn bread,
    Then, Brother, let me go.

Put me off at Crisfield,
    For the Shad are on the run.
And Hard Heads heading up the bay,
    To greet the springtime Sun.
And let me ramble round the docks,
    Where fishermen all smile.
And taste Shad and Hard Heads,
    Cooked in good old Crisfield Style.

The Crisfield Oyster Fleet

They are fixing up the skipjacks
    and the canoes by the score,
And the runboats jam the railways
    'till there's room for not one more.
They are rigging up the batteaus
    and the bugeyes white and neat,
As September brings a greeting
    to the Crisfield Oyster Fleet.

There's new tongs and culling hammers,
    new ropes all bright and strong.
There's new things of ev'ry manner,
    and in each heart a brand new song.
They are ready, they are waiting
    for old Tangier's tasty treat.
As September sings a greeting
    to the Crisfield Oyster Fleet.

From the many inland rivers
    soon you'll hear the motors hum
Through the stillness of the evening,
    loaded down as home they come.
For it's oyster time in Tangier
    and in Pocomoke's broad sweep
When September smiles a greeting
    to the Crisfield Oyster Fleet.

The Fishing Fair

They are coming down to Crisfield,
    from the valleys and the hills,
From the peaceful inland rivers, silvered
    lakes, and rippling rill;
They are coming from the cities,
    From the quaint old village streets
To where finny tribes are playing,
    where the sky and the water meets.

They are coming down to Crisfield,
    for a grand-old Fishing Fair;
To the Pocomoke so dreamy,
    with its splendors rich and rare.
They are coming down to Crisfield
    what a place to muse and dream!
They will fish in salty waters,
    in both sunlight and moonbeam.

Where wind is gently blowing,
    softly from a red-kissed dawn,
Here the human pulse beats longer;
    every heart is warm and strong.
They are coming, smiling, singing
    with a twinkle in each eye
Where a fellow's close to heaven,
    fishing 'neath old Tangier's sky.

Tangier Treat

There's a tonger in from Tangier,
    Brightened by the Tangier tide,
Bringing treats from Tangier waters,
    Where those luscious "Great Rocks" bide.
Get the 'barrows out , and roll 'em—suckers,
    Make those bright shells fly,
For I long to taste old Tangier,
    Salty Tangier 'neath the sky.

Yonder comes the skipjack "Mattie,"
    What a treat she has in store!
Followed by the canoe "Hattie,"
    Racing up the Tangier shore.
Chant the oyster song; yea sing it!
    Shout October's magic spell;
Let me be the first to taste them,
    For they've got the Tangier smell.

There's a tonger in from Tangier,
    And my heart just skips a beat,
And my mouth is all awater,
    Anxious for the Tangier treat.
Batteau, skipjack, skiff and canoe—
    Bright and spotless, old and new,
Tied up at the docks at sunset,
    Close by Tangier's magic blue.

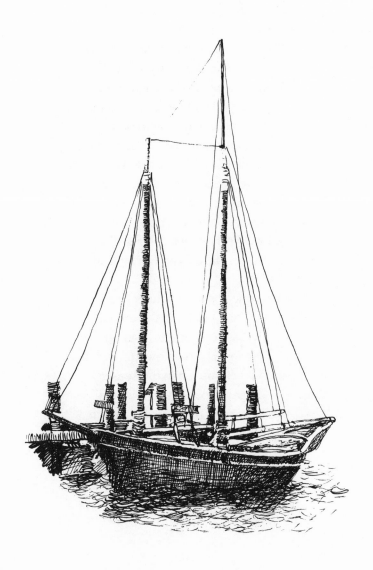

The Hard Crab Derby Ball

When your nerves are taut and frazzled
    And your skin begins to crawl,
When you get so darn disgusted
    That you want to end it all,
That's the time to start thinking
    It don't matter what you're worth
You're as good as any fellow
    That has ever been on earth.
Just let those nerves untangle
    There's a cure for one and all—
You will find it down in Crisfield
    At the Hard Crab Derby Ball.

Everyone is sure a winner
    Not one loser's in the crowd
For the mayor's got his sign up
    "No losers are allowed"
And I'll bet you when the season
    Comes around again next fall
You'll Be right there rootin', tootin',
    At the Hard Crab Derby Ball.

Tangier Magic

The crystal waves of Tangier
    Are playing round my feet,
The lazy clouds are drifting
    And the winds are cool and sweet.
A Fish Hawk circles high above
    The tranquil mirrored brine,
And starts my blood to tingling
    As if drunk with mellowed wine.

It sort o' fascinates me
    As the eastern sky aflame
Stirs my imagination
    And its beauty I acclaim.
I marvel as the colors fade away
    And reappear
Reflecting nature's magic
    On the bosom of Tangier.

There in the hazy distance
    Glitter miles of white sand bars,
While each grain seems to sparkle
    Just like diamond studded stars.
And yet there's something lacking
    Near the waters that lie blue
And something you would never guess,
    For that something is you.

(Dedicated to Sgt. Thomas W. Coulbourne,
Camp Chaffee, Arkansas.)

In This Sea Town When the Sun Sinks Low

There's a charm in this quaint sea-town
    With its narrow winding street,
At evening when the sun sinks low.
    And a pleasure to be found there
With old friends I long to meet,
    And live again those days of long ago.

Let me dream beside a railing,
    Let me marvel in a trance,
Let me vision ghost-ships sailing
    Splashed by waves that leap and dance.
Let me hear sea captains hailing
    From those ships of sweet romance,
In this sea-town when the sun sinks low.

There the winds are sweetly thickened
    By the river's scented breath,
As the lights begin to flash and glow.
    That still cause my pulse to quicken,
As the sun sinks in the West
    In this sea-town that I wish you'd know.

For those winds are sighing,
    As this town beside the sea
Hums its song that knows no dying
    Of its glories full and free.
Hums it 'til my soul is crying
    For the days that used to be
In this sea-town when the sun sinks low.

There is solitude and grandeur,
    When the purple shadows play
And the moonbeams touch the sea below.
    And a multitude of splendor
That no artist can portray
    No matter how much art that one may know.

For there're scenes that seem supernatural
    As I view the beauty there
And there's peace as nocturnal shadows fill the balmy air.
    And there's joy mine all eternal
Just to view the beauty rare,
    In this sea-town when the sun sinks low.

There is a charm in this quaint sea-town
    As old friends stop and greet
At evening when the sun sinks low.
    And a little bit of heaven
In its narrow, winding street,
    In the glory of the full moon's glow.

And I vision ghost-ships sailing
    With their side lights all ablaze
And I hear those songs still trailing
    Singing of those golden days.
As I glimpse the scene unveiling,
    All my heart is filled with praise,
In this sea-town when the sun sinks low.

13

Sailor's Paradise

There's a sailboat from Tangier
    Kissed by Tangier's magic dew
With her sides washed bright
    And shining by the spray.
Up for mystic fairy Tangier waters
    Rich in tint and hue,
I can get a glimpse of heaven night or day.

There's a sailboat, oh what visions
    That go racing through my mind,
As I lose myself in dreams so sweet and fair.
    Gazing there in sweet submission,
Ev'ry doubt and care behind, as I watch
    With heart stirred deep in silent prayer.

For it fills my ev'ry longing
    Just to feel the wet spray fly—
On my brow, and on my cheek and in my hair.
    In the glory of a dawning,
Underneath a Tangier sky.
    With the glory of sunrise everywhere.

There's a sailboat from Tangier,
    Haven of a sailor's dream.
And a paradise of joy to ev'ry breast.
    There is beauty in fair Tangier
Splashed with colors blue and green, when
    The winds have gently brushed its silv'ry crest.

Yes there's beauty in fair Tangier
    And there's romance by its shores
Where all worry and all trouble seen to cease
    On the bosom of old Tangier.
Let me dream there evermore,
    Where there's beauty, where there's joy,
And where there's peace.

Ghost Ships of Yesterday

Let's close our eyes and sail once more,
    down the fair Chesapeake
And listen to those side-wheels roar,
    our hearts too full to speak.
Where love and romance fill the air,
    each moonlit night, and day.
On board those ships so sweet and fair,
    whose ghosts still sail the bay.

Let's listen to those heart-felt songs,
    the deck-hands used to sing;
And hear the lighthouse bells ding-dong,
    and buoys as they ring.
To quide those dipping paddle wheels
    a churning through the foam.
To ports of splendor, mystic, real,
    the harbor lights of home.

There's Virgina, Maryland,
    Old Point Comfort, and the Sue.
The Talbot and the Corsica,
    that sailed the bay of blue.
The Eastern Shore and Pocomoke,
    the Cambridge white and fair.
The Rappahannock and Choptank,
    and also, dear Tangier,
Potomac, Joppa, Tolchester, Tivola
    and Dreamland;
The Rosedale and the Emma Giles,
    romantic names so grand.

Dear Helen and the sweet Louise,
    the Maggie, Tred Avon.
What sweeter names are there than these?
    or the fair Avalon?

There's many more of those dear ships,
    whose names we can't recall;
And many are the happy trips
    we had upon them all.
And many are the memories that make
    the heart strings yearn
For those dear ships that rest in peace,
    to never more return.

But still in fancy we can sail,
    and dream of flashing lights
In peace beside Ida's rail,
    and dear old Kitty Knight's.
Absorbed in memory's sweet dream,
    our hearts so light and gay
Upon those paddle wheels of steam
    Ghost Ships of yesterday.

The Dreamy Eastern Shore

If you're weary by your travels
    And your soul just longs for rest,
There's a place that bids you welcome,
    Where all hearts with joy are blest.
You have seen no place just like it,
    Tho' you've traveled the earth o'er.
Pack your grip, my friend, and hike it,
    To the Dreamy Eastern Shore.

You will meet the kind of people
    You have always longed to meet.
They will stop and bid you welcome
    With a smile sincere and sweet.
They will grip your hand, my brother,
    Like it never was before.
And you'll thank the Gods forever
    For this peaceful Eastern Shore.

It will fill your heart with gladness,
    If it should be blue or bare.
It will free your soul from sadness,
    With its scent of lilacs rare.
It will start your mind to dreaming
    Like it never did before
As you drink the magic beauty
    Of the fairy Eastern Shore.

So, if you are tired of roaming
    And your soul is black or blue.
Why not see this place of romance,
    That opens arms to you?
You'll rejoice to find the friendship
    That you've searched for the world o'er.
Pack your grip, you are all welcome,
    On the Eastern Shore.

All That I Ask

Give me a wind-swept storm beaten coast,
    pounded and lashed by the gale.
Watching the winging feathered host,
    the speck of an offshore sail;
Hearing the song of wild geese at night
    wafting their way from afar,
With naught to guide them in their flight,
    only the ray of a star.

Give me the roar of tumbling sea,
    upon a thundering shore;
And this is all I'll ask of thee,
    why should I ask for more?
There in a shanty, bathed in moon-beams,
    reflected by water's blue
Is all that I ask, lost in dreams
    for ever and ever with you.

2 On Ducking and Decoys

Time To Quit

The duck hunter was bewildered.
    He knew he was losing his mind.
For before him lay two pretty women
    Asleep in a duck blind.
Their lips were crimson with lipstick,
    Their eyes with mascara were black.
He knew if he had not gone crazy,
    At least he was on the right track.
For whenever a man finds two women
    In a duck blind with decoys out,
He better get home in a hurry
    And see if a doc is about.
For I am not taking no chances,
    And not one for pressing my luck.
But it's time that I quit,
    For I'm sure to get hit
When women start blasting at ducks.

(May 1, 1936.)

23

I'm Just an Old Decoy Duck

I'm just an old decoy duck
    made many years ago
By hands that have long left
    the scene
How many none can know.

I've laid in front of many a blind
    pelted by snow and rain
But now they have took me
    from the place I'll never be again.
They've set me me on a pedestal
    where I don't want to be
The only place I've ever known
    was on the lonely sea
Been rocked by blasts from
    many a gun as ducks went winging by
As northwest winds kicked up the sea
    and storm clouds filled the sky.
Here I sit in a room so warm
    locked by a bolted door
Won't someone throw me back again
    to my home by the river shore.

(This poem was discovered after Steve had died.)

24

The Drifter

I'm just an old has-been decoy.
    No ribbons have I won.
My sides and head are full of shot
    From many a blazing gun.

My home has been the river,
    Just drifting along with the tide.
No roof have I had for a shelter,
    No one place where I could abide.

I've rocked to winter's wild fury
    I've scorched in the heat of the sun.
I've drifted and drifted and drifted
    For tides never cease to run.

I was picked up by some fool collector
    Who put me up on a shelf.
But my place is out on the river
    Where I can drift all by myself.

I want to go back to the shoreline
    Where flying clouds hand thick and low.
And get the touch of the rain drops,
    And the velvety soft touch of the snow.

Are You the Best?

When you say you are the best
    At anything you do.
Just look around a little bit
    A surprise waits for you.
It's great to think you are the best
    But, keep it to yourself.
You'll find there is some right nice work
    On someone else's shelf.

An Old Decoy Duck

There is something about an old
    decoy duck.
One that you know is rare,
You treasure it like a mother would
    treasure her old rocking chair.

You picture it sitting by some
    windy shore
As the low flying clouds go
    sailing o'er.
You try and guess by whom
    it was made,
And how long ago it had been done.
But you can't find the answer
    though hard you may try,
Yet somehow it's been lots of fun.

You paint a picture
    of a wild, stormy day
Where the clouds flew by thick and low
And see that decoy in front
    warm, cozy room
And hear the guns as they roar and
    they boom,
While the nor'wester howls and
    winter has struck.
There is something about an old
    decoy duck.

The Old Duck Hunter

The old man stood in his shanty door,
    And looked at the storm clouds boiling o'er.
And said as the wind went by with a roar
    Gee! I'd like to be out there today.

The Old man's legs looked mighty weak,
    He was so old he could hardly speak.
And it looked like a tear trickled down his cheek,
    As he turned and walked away.

He had trod every foot of the marsh o'er and o'er,
    He knew every pebble and stone on the shore:
He had hunted it over back in days of yore.
    And memories piled high and deep.

He glanced at the decoys piled up on the floor.
    He looked at his gun he'd not need anymore.
Then he touched his old hunting coat near the door.
    He closed his eyes and went to sleep.

3 THE HOPELESS ROMANTIC

Mother

When God had finished everything,
    The land and the Oceans blue,
With song birds everywhere to sing,
    He thought of making you.
With Sun and Moon and Stars to shine
    And flowers' wondrous grace
'Twas incomplete, O' Mother mine
    Without your smiling face.

Your smiling face in childhood days
    With me tucked in your arms
Secure from childish fears that came
    And safe from worldly harm,
How eagerly I listened
    To those baby tales you told
As I nestled on your bosom
    With contentment in my soul.

Mother

I watched your face grow wrinkled,
    Dear, and saw time streak your hair.
I saw your form grow old and bent
    But love not lacking there.
How I watched with fear and trembling
    That was gripping at my heart
The day that soon was coming when
    We would have to part.

How I miss your good night kisses
    When my evening prayers were said,
How I miss those darling fingers as
    They tucked me safe in bed;
Thinking only of my comfort, asking God
    To keep me true,
And tonight, O precious Mother
    I am thinking most of you.

Thinking as the shadows gather softly
    Round my cabin door,
Thinking of a happy greeting
    When we meet to part no more,
Hoping, trusting, thru the twilight
    Praying as you did of yore,
We shall meet to know no parting
    On that happy golden shore.

Women

The old man said "women are sure queer animals that no man can figure out." They can do things a man would give his right arm to do, but he just can't even come close; for instance:

(1) Put a dozen men in a room everyone talking on a different subject, and know what all are saying.

(2) Read a book and listen to the radio at the same time and understand both.

(3) And this is the greatest of all. They can go to church Sunday morning, especially Easter Sunday, and tell you what every woman there is wearing from head to foot and be right. If you think you are smart try it sometime and you will wind up in an insane asylum.

Sure, "They shoot a lot of bull sometime," he said, "and who don't?"

But now they've took up shooting ducks, and we men are sure in danger of catching a load of buckshot some morning just before day.

But take it all in all, we just can't do without 'em. God bless 'em.

Don't Tease the Bees

Please don't tease the honeybees
    Don't let them take one sip.
If you do I'm telling you
    They'll make a million trips.
Flowers were made for honeybees
    That fly around the door.

Tulips are just sweet I know
    That bloom around your door.
But I've never tasted two lips yet
    That were half as sweet as yours.

Buckling Her Skates

The pond is again frozen over,
    And skaters with faces aglow
Are laughing and shouting and singing,
    Just like we did years ago.
The moon through the tree tops is beaming
    Down on the scene once again,
And starts all my fancy to dreaming
    And drifting down memory lane.
The years have been long, but old memories
    Come flooding tonight at their will,
And I'm buckling my old sweetheart's skates on,
    Bent down at her feet, by the hill.
And I still see the white tam-o-shanter
    That clung to her hair of spun gold,
As I silently buckled her skates on,
    With heart filled with love not untold.
And tonight I just sit here and wonder
    If sometimes in memory she strays
Back to the boy who buckled
    Her skates, and those long ago days.
And I wonder tonight who is kissing
    Those red lips that I used to know,
As I drift down that long lane of memory
    To those old days of long, long ago.

When Your Hair Has Turned To Silver

When your hair has turned to silver
And wrinkles start to sprout,
You can't read without glasses
And your hair starts falling out.
There's a garden filled with wire grass
Down the sunset trail we'll charge
I'll love you just the same dear
If you're bigger than a barge.

(Steve's parody on the song.)

Memory Lane

Song writers write and singers sing,
    Of memory lane when it's always spring.
When the time of year is always June,
    And every night there's a big full moon,
When the moonbeams danced on his old sweetheart's hair
    And perfume of roses filled the air.
He wonders and dreams where she is tonight,
    If her lips are as sweet, and her eyes as bright,
As they use to be those wonderful days
    When his mind was always in a haze.
So he wonders and dreams, ah, if he but knew.
    She was big as a tank and three feet through.
And the big strong guy that she can't forget,
    Don't weigh ninety pound, soaking wet.
And the funniest part of it all it seems,
    He never gets the girl of his dreams,
And she never wanted the one that she got.
    Old memory lane just isn't so hot.

37

Kitty's Branch

The pond by the woods is frozen over,
    And children with faces aglow
Are laughing and shouting and singing,
    The same as we did long ago.
And it starts my fancy to dreaming,
    And turns back the pages of time
When I was a lad on old Kitty's
    With that old sweetheart of mine.

I see her again in my vision;
    For visions of her always thrill.
As I bashfully bowed down beside her
    And buckled her skates by the hill.
I still feel the clasp of her fingers,
    And thrill at her laughing divine
When I was out skating on Kitty's
    With that old sweetheart of mine.

But now there's no skating on Kitty's
    For time has created a change.
And you'd never know it was Kitty's
    For it seems so lonely and strange.
The bushes and weeds and willows,
    Have filled in where it once was deep,
And some of the old gang of skaters
    Long since have been lying asleep.

And if tonight I had all the treasure
    Of earth, I would give it to find
That old Gang back there with their skates on
    And I with that old girl of mine.
Yet, still in my dreaming, their laughter
    I hear, and thrill with delight.
Tho' the years have been long, they're still with me
    Out skating on Kitty's tonight.

The Mules Are Out

By Johnny Whondoffer (Steve's pen name)

Somewhere near by "Jenkin's Creek",
    just at the break of day;
A lady went that morning quick
    to get the mules some hay.
But as she entered in the barn,
    glancing all about,
She saw that, to her great alarm
    the mules had gotten out.

Off she started to the place where
    her husband slept;
'Tho it was quite a distance off,
    right stealthily she crept,
Upon the porch and found the keys,
    while not one word was said,
She made the ladder with a bound,
    that came close to killing "Ed."

Then as she yelled out to him
    "both the mules are out!"
He was so taken unawares,
    he gave one awful shout.
It rumbled from the ditch bank,
    it rattled shanty town;
And from the bridge out to the edge
    of drowsy Tangier Sound.

Then to the top at last she stepped,
    or so the story goes,
She spied poor "Ed" there in the bed,
    Beside a wild eyed "Rose."
And with his heart still pounding,
    thought, "I have been one big fool,
She never would have caught me,
    had it not been for my mule."

Somewhere the sun is shining,
    and somewhere smiles are very thick,
There is a silver lining,
    but not near Jenkin's Creek.
And somewhere hearts are cheery,
    as they were down there no doubt,
Till along came Mary with the news,
    "Ed's" mules have gotten out.

(The incident actually happened. It created quite
a scandal in town. Steve used a pen name because
he didn't want Ed to get mad with him.)

Sunday Morning

I went to church Sunday morning,
　　To listen to the choir sing
And hear the music of the organ,
　　But I never heard a thing.

For you looked so sweet Sunday morning,
　　I never heard the choir at all.
I never heard them sing, or the church bell ring.
　　If I did I can't recall.

For you looked so sweet Sunday morning,
　　I couldn't keep my eyes off you.
And I'll he there again Sunday morning,
　　Praying that you'll be there too.

4 Poetic Commentary

The Jackpot!

When you have dumped the big jackpot
    and bask in the sunlight of fame.
When you gather in large sums of gold dust,
    just for the use of your name.
When they call you the most popular hero,
    whatever emerged from the track,
The world will sing out it's praises
    With the biggest slap on your back.
When the world asks for large donations,
    And brother, that's what it will do.
It will double and triple it's praises,
    And it's got you in a stew.
And then when your fame starts slipping
    And they've got you down to a small soul
They'll drop you just like a hot ingot
    and yell in your face. "You're a bum."

The Candidates

The candidates have started to yell,
    The voters they are going to tell
How big a crook his opponent is
    As if we didn't know their biz
And all that kind of stuff.
    We voted for their kind before,
But we are going to close the door
    And to the polls no more, no more.
We've simply had enough.

The T.V. Set !

Maybe you have often wondered
    If you'd live to be a hundred
Stop worrying, for it is one safe bet
    You will find all the answers.
Heart attacks and even cancer
    Can be cured by looking at your
T.V. set.

Money

Money is good, the old man said.
    If you enjoy it before you are dead.

What good is it when you come to your end
    And leave it for somebody else to spend.

The Bull Frog Band

The Bull Frog Band was in full, tune howling and growling at the moon.
     The big bass frog went Ooom Boom Boom; I marveled at his breath-
The sax frogs started getting all hot, all up and down that froggy lot,
     The bass drum frog was on the spot, and beat himself to death.
The fiddle frogs, those squealing pests, had done their very level best
     It seemed to me, to drown the rest. I hoped they would succeed.
And then the trombones got the pitch, and slid all over that frog ditch.
     The trumpet frogs then took the itch, and also took the lead.
And then I started in to cuss that panking, cranking, croacking, muss.
     Of orchestras, this was the wuss, of this I was quite sure.

Then something seemed to say to me, it won't be long until you see
     A very much worse orchestra, that should be unlawful?
And I just started wondering, just what it was, if anything,
     That could just play, or could just sing, anything more awful.
But I did not have long to go, for when I tuned my radio,
     Some wild eyed daffy maestro raised both arms in air;
Then with the wildest crash and din, so wild I almost felt the wind
     From all those horns of brass and tin, as they began to blare.
And now with Darwin I agree about his monkey theory.
     That men did hang down from a tree, and should hang there again.
They started with an overture, the worst of anything I'm sure
     That I had ever tried endure, or ever will again-
The big bass horn, as is his rule, would put to shame a braying mule.
     And blew like what he was, a fool. He had to be insane.
Then came the crying clarinet, and said you've not heard nothing yet,
     He blew it in ten seconds flat—What more can you expect?
And then the trombone guy got loose, altho I knew it was no use
     Still I would like to have a noose, and put it 'round his neck.
The bass drummer began to hum, and with a chilling yell he swung,
     And knocked the band clear thru his drum. Then they all took a fit.
And then I went right to the bogs, where I had cussed that band of frogs
     Because they groaned like dying dogs. Oh what a fool I've been.
To think that there just could not be, to want to hear and want to see
     A jazz band or an orchestra worse than I'd heard or seen.
But worse they are in time and sound, just take that frog band all around.
     They're better than those jazz mad hounds, with their groans and blaring.
But now at last I've found sweet rest, and I am rid of all these pests.
     And I am free of all this mess, and I am not now caring.
For never will I have to hear that tooting mess into my ear.
     And of them now I have no fear, you see, I've lost my hearing.

49

Here Lies Joe Racket

Here lies Joe Racket
In his wooden jacket
He kept neither horses or mules
He lived like a hog
He died like a dog
And left all his money to fools.

(We assume this is a head stone inscription
that Steve felt Joe Racket deserved.)

50

If

If there is nothing you can't do,
  And nothing you don't know,
No matter how hard it may be,
  You learned it long ago.
You mastered everything in sight,
  It was not hard at all;
You better look for a soft spot,
  You're headed for a fall.
Your head is bigger than your brain
  No question about that,
And you are going to have a job
  To find the right size hat.
You better start over again
  And head right back to school,
For everybody knows but you.
  That you're an ignorant fool.

Quotes

One thing sure, you'll never stumble on anything sitting down!

If you want the world to beat a path to your door, lay down and take a nap.

The average men's idea of a good sermon is one that goes over his head and hits his neighbor right between the eyes.

As a rule a man's a fool
When its hot, he wants it cool
When its cool, he wants it hot
He always wants what he ain't got.

5 VERSE ADVICE

A Greeting

When you are weary and lonely
    Wish there was someplace to go
To feel a slap on your shoulder.
    Someone to say hello
When you would be willing
    To walk a country mile
Just to have someone to greet you
    With a sincere happy smile.

Saints and Sinners

When some fellow yields to temptation
    And breaks a conventional law—
We look for no good in his make up
    But Lord how we look for a flaw.
No one asks "Who did the tempting?"
    Nor considers the battles he's fought.
His name becomes food for jackals.
    The saints who have never been caught.
I'm a sinner O lord, and I know it,
    I am weak and I stumble and fail
I am tossed on life's stormy ocean
    Like a ship that is tossed in a gale.
But I'm ready to accept the mercy
    And believe in the commandments though.
But deliver me lord from the judgement,
    Of the saints who have never been caught.

The Record I Keep

It isn't so much what my
    neighbor may think
Though I value his friendship a lot.
    It isn't some record they've
Written in ink
    That I want to keep free
From the blot
    It isn't some tale people whisper
About the way I gather myself.
    I want to keep evil and crookedness
Out of the record
    I keep for myself.

(Written on the bottom of a Canvasback
decoy by Lem in 1974. Steve never wrote
on the bottom of his decoys.)

A Cold Fact

To you who make the headlines,
     On this old earthly ball,
And gaze with pride and pleasure,
     At your trophies on the wall,
Remember, just remember,
     As you drink it way down deep,
No matter how you nail them down
     They won't forever keep.
For as sure as stars are shooting
     All around in outer space,
There's a kid down in the bush-league
     Coming on to take your place.
O it's great to hear the sheering
     Of the vast and mighty throng,
That sounds like distant thunder
     As it booms, and rolls along,
But the minute you start slipping
     They will laugh right in your face-
When the kid from out the bush-league
     Comes along and takes your place.

(Steve wrote this for a player on the Orioles.
It is not known if it was sent.)

Contentment

"How good God is to me," he said,
    "Although I have no mansion tall,
I have a shanty by the shore
    Where I can hear the wild goose call.
No wealth of fame I claim as mine.
    But just a lot of little things,
And when night comes I bow my head
    And realize I am a king."

Isn't it strange
That princess and kings,
And clowns that cape
In sawdust rings,
And common people
Like you and me
Are builders for eternity?
Each is given a bag of tools,
A shapeless mass,
A book of rules;
And each must make—
Ere life is flown—
A stumbling block
Or a steppingstone.

Isn't It Strange

Isn't it strange
That princesses and kings,
And clowns that caper
In sawdust rings,
And common people
Like you and me
Are builders for eternity?
Each is given a bag of tools,
A shapeless mass,
A book of rules;
And each must make,
Ere life is flown,
A stumbling block
Or a steppingstone.

There Is a Place

If you are tired and weary,
     And long some place to go,
To feel a glad hand on your shoulder
     To hear a voice say hello.

If you would be willing
     To walk a country mile,
Just to see a happy face
     And a cheery smile.

There is a place that's waiting
     For just such folk as you
Where hearts and doors are open
     To make your dreams come true.

6 THE LAST POEM

The Fishing Village

Its moonrise and shadows
    In ghostly silence creep
Captains of the village
    Sleep their last long sleep.

Lights long gone from windows
    Where houses used to be
That quided many a weary soul
    Back home from the sea.

No sound from the shoreline
    Except the pounding waves
Washing ever onward
    To the lonely graves.

Marsh grass inching onward
    In its relentless sweep
That soon will be ending
    As it seems to bow and weep.

Same old moon is shining
    As in days of yore
But the quaint old fishing village
    Is gone for evermore.

(This was the last poem written by Steve Ward.)

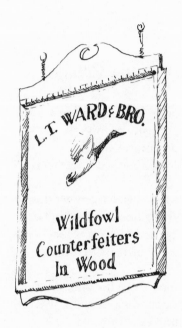

L. T. WARD & BRO.

Wildfowl
Counterfeiters
In Wood

Colophon

Editors: Ida Ward Linton, Don Briddell, and Jack Monday

Design: Jack Andrews
Typographic direction: Tom Bromley, Centre Grafik
Designed and composed on Macintosh computers using
Windsor normal and bold type.

Printing: Offset lithography by Sheridan Books on 55#
paper with symth sewn binding.

SkipJack Books

Orders for SkipJack books, are processed by the fulfillment service BookMasters.
All books and are shipped by UPS. Below is the current list of books.

Closed for Business, Ward
        Hard cover, 96 pages, reprinted 2001

Golden Age of Iron Work, Magaziner
        Hard cover, 224 pages, 2000

Samuel Yellin, Metalworker, Andrews
        Paper back, 144 pages, 2000

Colonial Wrought Iron, Plummer
        Hard cover, 256 pages, 1999

New Edge of the Anvil, Andrews
        Paper back, 256 pages, 1996

The Artist-Blacksmith's Craft, Schramm
        Hard cover, 156 pages, 1987
        Julius Schramm, a 24 page booklet is included

Contact BookMasters by the following methods:

call	1-800-247-6553
fax	1-419-281-6883
or on the web	www.bookmasters.com/skipjack/

 **SkipJack Press**
6 Laport Court
Ocean Pines, MD 21811

skipjack@ispchannel.com